The Key Facts™ on

Cambodia

Essential Information on Cambodia

By Patrick W. Nee

The Internationalist®

www.internationalist.com

The Internationalist®

International Business, Investment, and Travel

Published by:

The Internationalist Publishing Company

96 Walter Street/ Suite 200

Boston, MA 02131, USA

Tel: 617-354-7722

www.internationalist.com

PN@internationalist.com

Table Of Contents

Chapter 1: Background

Most Cambodians consider themselves to be Khmers,
descendants of the Angkor Empire that extended over
much of Southeast Asia and reached its zenith between the
10th and 13th centuries. Attacks by the Thai and Cham
(from present-day Vietnam) weakened the empire,
ushering in a long period of decline. The king placed the
country under French protection in 1863, and it became
part of French Indochina in 1887. Following Japanese
occupation in World War II, Cambodia gained full
independence from France in 1953. In April 1975, after a
five-year struggle, communist Khmer Rouge forces
captured Phnom Penh and evacuated all cities and towns.
At least 1.5 million Cambodians died from execution,
forced hardships, or starvation during the Khmer Rouge
regime under POL POT. A December 1978 Vietnamese
invasion drove the Khmer Rouge into the countryside,
began a 10-year Vietnamese occupation, and touched off
almost 13 years of civil war. The 1991 Paris Peace
Accords mandated democratic elections and a ceasefire,
which was not fully respected by the Khmer Rouge. UN-
sponsored elections in 1993 helped restore some
semblance of normalcy under a coalition government.
Factional fighting in 1997 ended the first coalition
government, but a second round of national elections in

1998 led to the formation of another coalition government and renewed political stability. The remaining elements of the Khmer Rouge surrendered in early 1999. Some of the surviving Khmer Rouge leaders have been tried or are awaiting trial for crimes against humanity by a hybrid UN-Cambodian tribunal supported by international assistance. Elections in July 2003 were relatively peaceful, but it took one year of negotiations between contending political parties before a coalition government was formed. In October 2004, King Norodom SIHANOUK abdicated the throne and his son, Prince Norodom SIHAMONI, was selected to succeed him. Local elections were held in Cambodia in April 2007, with little of the pre-election violence that preceded prior elections. National elections in July 2008 were relatively peaceful, as were commune council elections in June 2012.

Chapter 2: Geography

Location:

Southeastern Asia, bordering the Gulf of Thailand, between Thailand, Vietnam, and Laos

Geographic coordinates:

13 00 N, 105 00 E

Map references:

Southeast Asia

Area:

total: 181,035 sq km

country comparison to the world: 90

land: 176,515 sq km

water: 4,520 sq km

Area - comparative:

slightly smaller than Oklahoma

Land boundaries:

total: 2,572 km

border countries: Laos 541 km, Thailand 803 km, Vietnam 1,228 km

Coastline:

443 km

Maritime claims:

    territorial sea: 12 nm

    contiguous zone: 24 nm

    exclusive economic zone: 200 nm

    continental shelf: 200 nm

Climate:

    tropical; rainy, monsoon season (May to November); dry season (December to April); little seasonal temperature variation

Terrain:

    mostly low, flat plains; mountains in southwest and north

Elevation extremes:

    lowest point: Gulf of Thailand 0 m

    highest point: Phnum Aoral 1,810 m

Natural resources:

    oil and gas, timber, gemstones, iron ore, manganese, phosphates, hydropower potential

Land use:

    arable land: 22.09%

    permanent crops: 0.86%

    other: 77.05% (2011)

Irrigated land:

    3,536 sq km (2006)

Total renewable water resources:

    476.1 cu km (2011)

Freshwater withdrawal (domestic/industrial/agricultural):

total: 2.18 cu km/yr (4%/2%/94%)

per capita: 159.8 cu m/yr (2006)

Natural hazards:

monsoonal rains (June to November); flooding; occasional droughts

Environment - current issues:

illegal logging activities throughout the country and strip mining for gems in the western region along the border with Thailand have resulted in habitat loss and declining biodiversity (in particular, destruction of mangrove swamps threatens natural fisheries); soil erosion; in rural areas, most of the population does not have access to potable water; declining fish stocks because of illegal fishing and overfishing

Environment - international agreements:

party to: Biodiversity, Climate Change, Climate Change-Kyoto Protocol, Desertification, Endangered Species, Hazardous Wastes, Marine Life Conservation, Ozone Layer Protection, Ship Pollution, Tropical Timber 94, Wetlands, Whaling

signed, but not ratified: Law of the Sea

Geography - note:

a land of paddies and forests dominated by the Mekong River and Tonle Sap (Southeast Asia's largest freshwater lake)

Chapter 3: People and Society

Nationality:

> <u>noun</u>: Cambodian(s)

> <u>adjective</u>: Cambodian

Ethnic groups:

> Khmer 90%, Vietnamese 5%, Chinese 1%, other 4%

Languages:

> Khmer (official) 96.3%, other 3.7% (2008 est.)

Religions:

> Buddhist (official) 96.9%, Muslim 1.9%, Christian 0.4%,
> other 0.8% (2008 est.)

Population:

> 15,458,332 (July 2014 est.)

> <u>country comparison to the world</u>: 69

Age structure:

> <u>0-14 years</u>: 31.6% (male 2,460,659/female 2,423,619)

> <u>15-24 years</u>: 20.5% (male 1,565,135/female 1,596,099)

> <u>25-54 years</u>: 38.9% (male 2,938,366/female 3,082,496)

> <u>55-64 years</u>: 4% (male 298,733/female 482,588)

> <u>65 years and over</u>: 3.9% (male 229,684/female 380,953)
> (2014 est.)

Dependency ratios:

> total dependency ratio: 57.3 %
>
> youth dependency ratio: 48.9 %
>
> elderly dependency ratio: 8.4 %
>
> potential support ratio: 11.9 (2013)

Median age:

> total: 24.1 years
>
> male: 23.4 years
>
> female: 24.8 years (2014 est.)

Population growth rate:

> 1.63% (2014 est.)
>
> country comparison to the world: 75

Birth rate:

> 24.4 births/1,000 population (2014 est.)
>
> country comparison to the world: 60

Death rate:

> 7.78 deaths/1,000 population (2014 est.)
>
> country comparison to the world: 108

Net migration rate:

> -0.32 migrant(s)/1,000 population (2014 est.)
>
> country comparison to the world: 127

Urbanization:

> urban population: 20% of total population (2011)
>
> rate of urbanization: 2.13% annual rate of change (2010-15 est.)

Major urban areas - population:

PHNOM PENH (capital) 1.55 million (2011)

Sex ratio:

at birth: 1.05 male(s)/female

0-14 years: 1.02 male(s)/female

15-24 years: 0.98 male(s)/female

25-54 years: 0.95 male(s)/female

55-64 years: 0.94 male(s)/female

65 years and over: 0.6 male(s)/female

total population: 0.94 male(s)/female (2014 est.)

Mother's mean age at first birth:

22.8

note: median age at first birth among women 25-29 (2010 est.)

Maternal mortality rate:

250 deaths/100,000 live births (2010)

country comparison to the world: 45

Infant mortality rate:

total: 51.36 deaths/1,000 live births

country comparison to the world: 36

male: 58.1 deaths/1,000 live births

female: 44.31 deaths/1,000 live births (2014 est.)

Life expectancy at birth:

>total population: 63.78 years
>
>country comparison to the world: 179
>
>male: 61.35 years
>
>female: 66.32 years (2014 est.)

Total fertility rate:

>2.66 children born/woman (2014 est.)
>
>country comparison to the world: 74

Contraceptive prevalence rate:

>50.5% (2010/11)

Health expenditures:

>5.7% of GDP (2011)
>
>country comparison to the world: 118

Physicians density:

>0.23 physicians/1,000 population (2008)

Hospital bed density:

>0.7 beds/1,000 population (2011)

Drinking water source:

>improved:
>
>>*urban*: 89.6% of population
>>
>>*rural*: 61.5% of population
>>
>>*total*: 67.1% of population
>
>unimproved:
>
>>*urban*: 10.4% of population
>>
>>*rural*: 38.5% of population
>>
>>*total*: 32.9% of population (2011 est.)

Sanitation facility access:

>improved:

>>*urban*: 76.4% of population

>>*rural*: 22.3% of population

>>*total*: 33.1% of population

>unimproved:

>>*urban*: 23.6% of population

>>*rural*: 77.7% of population

>>*total*: 66.9% of population (2011 est.)

HIV/AIDS - adult prevalence rate:

>0.8% (2012 est.)

>country comparison to the world: 53

HIV/AIDS - people living with HIV/AIDS:

>76,400 (2012 est.)

>country comparison to the world: 50

HIV/AIDS - deaths:

>2,700 (2012 est.)

>country comparison to the world: 54

Major infectious diseases:

>degree of risk: very high

>food or waterborne diseases: bacterial diarrhea, hepatitis A, and typhoid fever

>vectorborne diseases: dengue fever, Japanese encephalitis, and malaria

note: highly pathogenic H5N1 avian influenza has been identified in this country; it poses a negligible risk with extremely rare cases possible among US citizens who have close contact with birds (2013)

Obesity - adult prevalence rate:

2.1% (2008)

country comparison to the world: 183

Children under the age of 5 underweight:

29% (2011)

country comparison to the world: 20

Education expenditures:

2.6% of GDP (2010)

country comparison to the world: 152

Literacy:

definition: age 15 and over can read and write

total population: 73.9%

male: 82.8%

female: 65.9% (2009 est.)

School life expectancy (primary to tertiary education):

total: 11 years

male: 12 years

female: 10 years (2008)

Child labor – children ages 5-14:

total number: 1,345,269

percentage: 39 % (2001 est.)

Unemployment, youth ages 15-24:

    total: 3.4%

    country comparison to the world: 141

    male: 3.5%

    female: 3.3% (2008)

Chapter 4: Government and Key Leaders

Country name:

> conventional long form: Kingdom of Cambodia
>
> conventional short form: Cambodia
>
> local long form: Preahreacheanachakr Kampuchea
> (phonetic pronunciation)
>
> local short form: Kampuchea
>
> former: Khmer Republic, Democratic Kampuchea,
> People's Republic of Kampuchea, State of Cambodia

Government type:

> multiparty democracy under a constitutional monarchy

Capital:

> name: Phnom Penh
>
> geographic coordinates: 11 33 N, 104 55 E
>
> time difference: UTC+7 (12 hours ahead of Washington,
> DC during Standard Time)

Administrative divisions:

> 23 provinces (khett, singular and plural) and 1
> municipality (krong, singular and plural)
>
> provinces: Banteay Meanchey, Battambang, Kampong
> Cham, Kampong Chhnang, Kampong Speu, Kampong
> Thom, Kampot, Kandal, Kep, Koh Kong, Kratie,
> Mondolkiri, Oddar Meanchey, Pailin, Preah Vihear, Prey
> Veng, Pursat, Ratanakiri, Siem Reap, Sihanoukville, Stung
> Treng, Svay Rieng, Takeo

municipalities: Phnom Penh (Phnum Penh)

Independence:

9 November 1953 (from France)

National holiday:

Independence Day, 9 November (1953)

Constitution:

previous 1947; latest promulgated 21 September 1993; amended 1999, 2008 (2008)

Legal system:

civil law system (influenced by the UN Transitional Authority in Cambodia) customary law, Communist legal theory, and common law

International law organization participation:

accepts compulsory ICJ jurisdiction with reservations; accepts ICCt jurisdiction

Suffrage:

18 years of age; universal

Executive branch:

chief of state: King Norodom SIHAMONI (since 29 October 2004) head of government: Prime Minister HUN SEN (since 14 January 1985) [co-prime minister from 1993 to 1997]; Permanent Deputy Prime Minister MEN SAM AN (since 25 September 2008); Deputy Prime Ministers SAR KHENG (since 3 February 1992); SOK AN, TEA BANH, HOR NAMHONG, NHEK BUNCHHAY (since 16 July 2004); BIN CHHIN (since 5 September 2007); KEAT CHHON, YIM CHHAI LY (since 24 September 2008); KE KIMYAN (since 12 March 2009)

cabinet: Council of Ministers named by the prime minister and appointed by the monarch

elections: the king chosen by a Royal Throne Council from among all eligible males of royal descent; following legislative elections, a member of the majority party or majority coalition named prime minister by the Chairman of the National Assembly and appointed by the king

Legislative branch:

bicameral, consists of the Senate (61 seats; 2 members appointed by the monarch, 2 elected by the National Assembly, and 57 elected by parliamentarians and commune councils; members serve five-year terms) and the National Assembly (123 seats; members elected by popular vote to serve five-year terms)

elections: Senate - last held on 4 February 2012 (next to be held in February 2018); National Assembly - last held on 28 July 2013 (next to be held in July 2018) election results: Senate - percent of vote by party - CPP 77.8%, CNRP (SRP) 22.2%; seats by party - CPP 46, CNRP (SRP) 11; National Assembly - percent of vote by party - CPP 48.8%, NRP 44.5%, FUNCINPEC 3.9%, others 2.8%; seats by party - CPP 68, CNRP 55

Judicial branch:

Highest court(s): Supreme Court (organized into 5- and 9-judge panels and includes a court chief and deputy chief); Constitutional Court (consists of 9 members)

note: in 1997, the Cambodian Government requested UN assistance in establishing trials to prosecute former Khmer Rouge senior leaders for crimes against humanity committed during the 1975-1979 Khmer Rouge regime; the Extraordinary Chambers of the Courts in Cambodia were established and began hearings for the first case in 2009

Judge selection and term of offfice: Supreme Court and Constitutional Court judge candidates recommended by the Supreme Council of Magistracy, a 9-member body chaired by the monarch and includes other high-level judicial officers; judges of both courts appointed by the monarch; Supreme Court judge tenure NA; Constitutional Court judges appointed for 9-year terms with one-third of the court renewed every 3 years

subordinate courts: municipal and provincial courts; appellate courts; military court

Political parties and leaders:

Cambodian People's Party or CPP [CHEA SIM]

Cambodian National Rescue Party or CNRP [SAM RANGSI also spelled SAM RAINSY]

National United Front for an Independent, Neutral, Peaceful, and Cooperative Cambodia or FUNCINPEC [KEV PUT REAKSMEI]

Nationalist Party or NP former Norodom Ranariddh Party or NRP [SAO RANY]

note: the CNRP is a merger between the former Human Rights Party or HRP [KHEM SOKHA, also spelled KEM SOKHA] and the Sam Rangsi Party or SRP

Political pressure groups and leaders:

Cambodian Freedom Fighters or CFF

Partnership for Transparency Fund or PTF (anti-corruption organization)

Students Movement for Democracy

The Committee for Free and Fair Elections or Comfrel

other: human rights organizations; vendors

International organization participation:

ADB, ARF, ASEAN, CICA, CICA (observer), EAS, FAO, G-77, IAEA, IBRD, ICAO, ICRM, IDA, IFAD, IFC, IFRCS, ILO, IMF, IMO, Interpol, IOC, IOM, IPU, ISO (correspondent), ITU, MINUSMA, MIGA, NAM, OIF, OPCW, PCA, UN, UNCTAD, UNESCO, UNIDO,

UNIFIL, UNMISS, UNWTO, UPU, WCO, WFTU
(NGOs), WHO, WIPO, WMO, WTO

Diplomatic representation in the US:

chief of mission: Ambassador HENG HEM (since 29
January 2009)

chancery: 4530 16th Street NW, Washington, DC 20011

telephone: [1] (202) 726-7742

FAX: [1] (202) 726-8381

Diplomatic representation from the US:

chief of mission: Ambassador William E. TODD (since 17
April 2012)

embassy: #1, Street 96, Sangkat Wat Phnom, Khan Daun
Penh, Phnom Penh

mailing address: Box P, APO AP 96546

telephone: [855] (23) 728-000

FAX: [855] (23) 728-600

Key Leaders:

King	Norodom SIHAMONI
Prime Min.	HUN SEN
Permanent Dep. Prime Min.	MEN SAM AN
Dep. Prime Min.	BIN CHHIN
Dep. Prime Min.	HOR NAMHONG
Dep. Prime Min.	KE KIMYAN
Dep. Prime Min.	KEAT CHHON
Dep. Prime Min.	NHEK BUNCHHAY
Dep. Prime Min.	SAR KHENG
Dep. Prime Min.	SOK AN
Dep. Prime Min.	TEA BANH, *Gen.*

Dep. Prime Min.	YIM CHHAI LY
Min. of the Office of the Council of Ministers	SOK AN
Min. of Agriculture, Forestry, & Fisheries	OUK RABUN
Min. of Commerce	SUN CHANTHOL
Min. of Cults & Religious Affairs	MIN KHIN
Min. of Culture & Fine Arts	PHOEUNG SAKONA
Min. of Economy & Finance	AUN PORN MONIROTH
Min. of Education, Youth, & Sport	HANG CHUON NARON
Min. of Environment	SAY SAMAL
Min. of Foreign Affairs & Intl. Cooperation	HOR NAMHONG
Min. of Health	MAM BUN HENG
Min. of Industry, Mines, & Energy	CHAM PRASIDH
Min. of Information	KHIEU KANHARITH
Min. of Interior	SAR KHENG
Min. of Justice	ANG VONG VATTANA
Min. of Labor & Vocational Training	ITH SAM HENG
Min. of Land Management, Urbanization, & Construction	IM CHHUN LIM
Min. of National Defense	TEA BANH, *Gen.*
Min. of Planning	CHHAY THAN
Min. of Posts & Telecommunications	PRAK SOKHONN
Min. of Public Works & Transportation	TRAM IV TOEK
Min. of Relations With the National Assembly, Senate, & Inspection	MEN SAM AN
Min. of Rural Development	CHEA SOPHARA
Min. of Social Affairs, War Veterans, & Youth Rehabilitation	VORNG SAUT
Min. of Tourism	THONG KHON

Min. of Water Resources & Meteorology	LIM KEAN-HAO
Min. of Women's Affairs	Ing Kantha PHAVI, *Dr.*
Governor, State Bank	CHEA CHANTO
Ambassador to the US	HEM HENG
Permanent Representative to the UN, New York	TUY RY

Flag description:

three horizontal bands of blue (top), red (double width), and blue with a white three-towered temple representing Angkor Wat outlined in black in the center of the red band; red and blue are traditional Cambodian colors

note: only national flag to incorporate an actual building in its design

National symbol(s):

Angkor Wat temple; kouprey (wild ox)

National anthem:

name: "Nokoreach" (Royal Kingdom)

lyrics/music: CHUON NAT/F. PERRUCHOT and J. JEKYLL

note: adopted 1941, restored 1993; the anthem, based on a Cambodian folk tune, was restored after the defeat of the Communist regime

Chapter 5: Economy

Economy - overview:

Since 2004, garments, construction, agriculture, and tourism have driven Cambodia's growth. GDP climbed more than 7% per year between 2010 and 2013. The garment industry currently employs more about 400,000 people and accounts for about 70% of Cambodia's total exports. In 2005, exploitable oil deposits were found beneath Cambodia's territorial waters, representing a potential revenue stream for the government, if commercial extraction becomes feasible. Mining also is attracting some investor interest and the government has touted opportunities for mining bauxite, gold, iron and gems. The tourism industry has continued to grow rapidly with foreign arrivals exceeding 2 million per year since 2007 and reaching over 3 million visitors in 2012. Cambodia, nevertheless, remains one of the poorest countries in Asia and long-term economic development remains a daunting challenge, inhibited by endemic corruption, limited educational opportunities, high income inequality, and poor job prospects. Approximately 4 million people live on less than $1.25 per day, and 37% of Cambodian children under the age of 5 suffer from chronic malnutrition. More than 50% of the population is less than 25 years old. The population lacks education and productive skills, particularly in the impoverished countryside, which also lacks basic infrastructure. The Cambodian Government is working with bilateral and multilateral donors, including the Asian Development Bank, the World Bank and IMF, to address the country's many pressing needs; more than 50% of the government budget comes from donor assistance. The major economic challenge for Cambodia over the next decade will be fashioning an economic environment in which the private sector can create enough jobs to handle Cambodia's demographic imbalance.

GDP (purchasing power parity):

$39.64 billion (2013 est.)

country comparison to the world: 107

$37.04 billion (2012 est.)

$34.52 billion (2011 est.)

note: data are in 2013 US dollars

GDP (official exchange rate):

$15.64 billion (2013 est.)

GDP - real growth rate:

7% (2013 est.)

country comparison to the world: 21

7.3% (2012 est.)

7.1% (2011 est.)

GDP - per capita (PPP):

$2,600 (2013 est.)

country comparison to the world: 183

$2,400 (2012 est.)

$2,300 (2011 est.)

note: data are in 2013 US dollars

Gross national saving:

9.6% of GDP (2013 est.)

country comparison to the world: 138

9.1% of GDP (2012 est.)

12% of GDP (2011 est.)

GDP – composition, by end use:

household consumption: 74.7%

government consumption: 7.7%

investment in fixed capital: 16.4%

investment in inventories: 2.1%

exports of goods and services: 65.3%

imports of goods and services: -66.2% (2013 est.)

GDP - composition by sector:

agriculture: 34.8%

industry: 24.5%

services: 40.7% (2013 est.)

Agriculture – products:

rice, rubber, corn, vegetables, cashews, cassava (manioc), silk

Industries:

> tourism, garments, construction, rice milling, fishing, wood and wood products, rubber, cement, gem mining, textiles

Industrial production growth rate:

> 9.5% (2013 est.)
>
> country comparison to the world: 17

Labor force:

> 7.9 million (2011 est.)
>
> country comparison to the world: 60

Labor force - by occupation:

> agriculture: 55.8%
>
> industry: 16.9%
>
> services: 27.3% (2010 est.)

Unemployment rate:

> 0% (2011 est.)
>
> country comparison to the world: 1
>
> 0.3% (2010 est.)

Population below poverty line:

> 20% (2012 est.)

Household income or consumption by percentage share:

> lowest 10%: 3%
>
> highest 10%: 37.3% (2007)

Distribution of family income - Gini index:

37.9 (2008 est.)

country comparison to the world: 73

41.9 (2004 est.)

Budget:

revenues: $2.685 billion

expenditures: $3.1 billion (2013 est.)

Taxes and other revenues:

17.2% of GDP (2013 est.)

country comparison to the world: 181

Budget surplus (+) or deficit (-):

-2.7% of GDP (2013 est.)

country comparison to the world: 111

Public Debt:

NA% of GDP

Inflation rate (consumer prices):

3.2% (2013 est.)

country comparison to the world: 118

2.9% (2012 est.)

Central bank discount rate:

NA% (31 December 2012)

country comparison to the world: 68

5.25% (31 December 2007)

Commercial bank prime lending rate:

13% (31 December 2013 est.)

country comparison to the world: 61

12.98% (31 December 2012 est.)

Stock of narrow money:

$1.206 billion (31 December 2013 est.)

country comparison to the world: 145

$995.1 million (31 December 2012 est.)

Stock of broad money:

$8.373 billion (31 December 2013 est.)

country comparison to the world: 109

$7.1 billion (31 December 2012 est.)

Stock of domestic credit:

$5.705 billion (31 December 2013 est.)

country comparison to the world: 112

$4.801 billion (31 December 2012 est.)

Current account balance:

-$1.262 billion (2013 est.)

country comparison to the world: 126

-$1.208 billion (2012 est.)

Exports:

$6.781 billion (2013 est.)

country comparison to the world: 104

$6.016 billion (2012 est.)

Exports - commodities:

clothing, timber, rubber, rice, fish, tobacco, footwear

Exports - partners:

US 32.6%, UK 8.3%, Germany 7.7%, Canada 7.7%,
Singapore 6.6%, Vietnam 5.7%, Japan 4.7% (2012)

Imports:

$8.895 billion (2013 est.)

country comparison to the world: 106

$7.965 billion (2012 est.)

Imports - commodities:

petroleum products, cigarettes, gold, construction
materials, machinery, motor vehicles, pharmaceutical
products

Imports - partners:

Thailand 27.1%, Vietnam 20.3%, China 19.5%, Singapore
7.1%, Hong Kong 5.8%, South Korea 4.3% (2012)

Reserves of foreign exchange and gold:

$5.415 billion (31 December 2013 est.)

country comparison to the world: 93

$4.938 billion (31 December 2012 est.)

Debt - external:

$4.912 billion (31 December 2013 est.)

country comparison to the world: 123

$4.567 billion (31 December 2012 est.)

Exchange rates:

riels (KHR) per US dollar -

4,037.6 (2013 est.)

4,033 (2012 est.)

4,184.9 (2010 est.)

4,139 (2009)

4,070.94 (2008)

Chapter 6: Energy

Electricity - production:

> 1.019 billion kWh (2011 est.)

> country comparison to the world: 144

Electricity - consumption:

> 2.573 billion kWh (2011 est.)

> country comparison to the world: 134

Electricity - exports:

> 0 kWh (2012 est.)

> country comparison to the world: 113

Electricity - imports:

> 1.83 billion kWh (2011 est.)

> country comparison to the world: 55

Electricity - installed generating capacity:

> 359,900 kW (2010 est.)

> country comparison to the world: 148

Electricity - from fossil fuels:

> 94.8% of total installed capacity (2010 est.)

> country comparison to the world: 69

Electricity - from nuclear fuels:

> 0% of total installed capacity (2010 est.)

> country comparison to the world: 59

Electricity - from hydroelectric plants:

> 3.6% of total installed capacity (2010 est.)

> country comparison to the world: 126

Electricity - from other renewable sources:

1.6% of total installed capacity (2010 est.)

country comparison to the world: 76

Crude oil - production:

0.5 bbl/day (2012 est.)

country comparison to the world: 132

Crude oil - exports:

0 bbl/day (2010 est.)

country comparison to the world: 94

Crude oil - imports:

0 bbl/day (2010 est.)

country comparison to the world: 168

Crude oil - proved reserves:

0 bbl (1 January 2013 es)

country comparison to the world: 113

Refined petroleum products - production:

0 bbl/day (2010 est.)

country comparison to the world: 128

Refined petroleum products - consumption:

39,350 bbl/day (2011 est.)

country comparison to the world: 108

Refined petroleum products - exports:

0 bbl/day (2010 est.)

country comparison to the world: 160

Refined petroleum products - imports:

26,250 bbl/day (2010 est.)

country comparison to the world: 96

Natural gas - production:

0 cu m (2011 est.)

country comparison to the world: 110

Natural gas - consumption:

0 cu m (2010 est.)

country comparison to the world: 126

Natural gas - exports:

0 cu m (2011 est.)

country comparison to the world: 74

Natural gas - imports:

0 cu m (2011 est.)

country comparison to the world: 169

Natural gas - proved reserves:

0 cu m (1 January 2013 es)

country comparison to the world: 120

Carbon dioxide emissions from consumption of energy:

4.39 million Mt (2011 est.)

country comparison to the world: 130

Chapter 7: Communications

Telephones - main lines in use:

584,000 (2012)

country comparison to the world: 93

Telephones - mobile cellular:

19.1 million (2012)

country comparison to the world: 53

Telephone system:

general assessment: adequate fixed-line and/or cellular service in Phnom Penh and other provincial cities; mobile-cellular phone systems are widely used in urban areas to bypass deficiencies in the fixed-line network; mobile-phone coverage is rapidly expanding in rural areas

domestic: ixed-line connections stand at about 4 per 100 persons; mobile-cellular usage, aided by competition among service providers, is increasing rapidly and stands at 92 per 100 persons

international: country code - 855; adequate but expensive landline and cellular service available to all countries from Phnom Penh and major provincial cities; satellite earth station - 1 Intersputnik (Indian Ocean region) (2011)

Broadcast media:

mixture of state-owned, joint public-private, and privately owned broadcast media; 9 TV broadcast stations with most operating on multiple channels, including 1 state-operated station broadcasting from multiple locations, 6 stations either jointly operated or privately owned with some broadcasting from several locations, and 2 TV relay stations - one relaying a French TV station and the other relaying a Vietnamese TV station; multi-channel cable and satellite systems are available; roughly 50 radio broadcast stations - 1 state-owned broadcaster with multiple stations and a large mixture of public and private broadcasters; several international broadcasters are available (2009)

Internet country code:

.kh

Internet hosts:

13,784 (2012)

country comparison to the world: 129

Internet users:

78,500 (2009)

country comparison to the world: 167

Chapter 8: Transportation

Airports:

    16 (2013)

    country comparison to the world: 142

Airports - with paved runways:

    total: 6

    2,438 to 3,047 m: 3

    1,524 to 2,437 m: 2

    914 to 1,523 m: 1 (2013)

Airports - with unpaved runways:

    total: 10

    1,524 to 2,437 m: 2

    914 to 1,523 m: 7

    under 914 m: 1 (2013)

Heliports:

    1 (2013)

Railways:

    total: 690 km

    country comparison to the world: 101

    narrow gauge: 690 km 1.000-m gauge

    note: under restoration (2010)

Roadways:

> total: 39,618 km
>
> country comparison to the world: 88
>
> paved: 2,492 km
>
> unpaved: 37,126 km (2009)

Waterways:

> 3,700 km (mainly on Mekong River) (2012)
>
> country comparison to the world: 29

Merchant marine:

> total: 544
>
> country comparison to the world: 21
>
> by type: bulk carrier 38, cargo 459, carrier 7, chemical tanker 4, container 4, liquefied gas 1, passenger 1, passenger/cargo 6, petroleum tanker 8, refrigerated cargo 11, roll on/roll off 4, vehicle carrier 1
>
> foreign-owned: 352 (Belgium 1, Canada 2, China 177, Cyprus 4, Egypt 4, Estonia 1, French Polynesia 1, Gabon 1, Greece 2, Hong Kong 10, Indonesia 2, Ireland 1, Japan 1, Lebanon 5, Russia 50, Singapore 3, South Korea 10, Syria 22, Taiwan 1, Turkey 15, UAE 2, UK 1, Ukraine 35, Vietnam 1) (2010)

Ports and terminals:

> major seaport(s): Sihanoukville (Kampong Saom)
>
> river port(s): Phnom Penh (Mekong)

Chapter 9: Military

Military branches:

>Royal Cambodian Armed Forces: Royal Cambodian Army, Royal Khmer Navy, Royal Cambodian Air Force (2013)

Military service age and obligation:

>18 is the legal minimum age for compulsory and voluntary military service (2012)

Manpower available for military service:

>males age 16-49: 3,883,724

>females age 16-49: 4,003,585 (2010 est.)

Manpower fit for military service:

>males age 16-49: 2,638,167

>females age 16-49: 2,965,328 (2010 est.)

Manpower reaching militarily significant age annually:

>male: 151,143

>female: 154,542 (2010 est.)

Military expenditures:

>1.54% of GDP (2012)

>country comparison to the world: 60

>1.5% of GDP (2011)

>1.54% of GDP (2010)

Chapter 10: Transnational Issues

Disputes - international:

Cambodia is concerned about Laos' extensive upstream dam construction; Cambodia and Thailand dispute sections of boundary; in 2011 Thailand and Cambodia resorted to arms in the dispute over the location of the boundary on the precipice surmounted by Preah Vihear Temple ruins, awarded to Cambodia by ICJ decision in 1962 and part of a UN World Heritage site; Cambodia accuses Vietnam of a wide variety of illicit cross-border activities; progress on a joint development area with Vietnam is hampered by an unresolved dispute over sovereignty of offshore islands

Trafficking in persons:

current situatino: Cambodia is a source, transit, and destination country for men, women, and children subjected to forced labor and sex trafficking; Cambodian men, women, and children migrate to countries within the region for legitimate work but are subsequently subjected to sex trafficking, domestic servitude, debt bondage, or forced labor; the inability to understand formal obligations, read contracts, or pay processing fees, and inadequate government regulatory oversight renders some Cambodian migrant workers vulnerable to such exploitation; poor Cambodian children are subject to forced labor, including forced begging in Thailand and Vietnam; Cambodian and ethnic Vietnamese women and girls are trafficked from rural areas to urban centers for sexual exploitation; Cambodian men are the main exploiters of child prostitutes, but men from other Asian countries, the US, and Europe travel to Cambodia for child sex tourism

<u>tier rating:</u> Tier 2 Watch List - Cambodia does not fully comply with the minimum standards for the elimination of trafficking; however, it is making significant efforts to do so; the government has prosecuted and convicted fewer trafficking offenders and identified fewer victims than in the previous year; corruption continues to impede anti-trafficking endeavors; authorities systematically refer identified victims to NGO shelters, which provide the majority of services but lack long-term care services, making victims, particularly children, vulnerable to re-trafficking; the government has established a migration working group within its anti-trafficking committee to better address the exploitation of Cambodian workers abroad, but laws governing migrant workers abroad remain weak (2013)

Illicit drugs:

narcotics-related corruption reportedly involving some in the government, military, and police; limited methamphetamine production; vulnerable to money laundering due to its cash-based economy and porous borders

Map of Cambodia

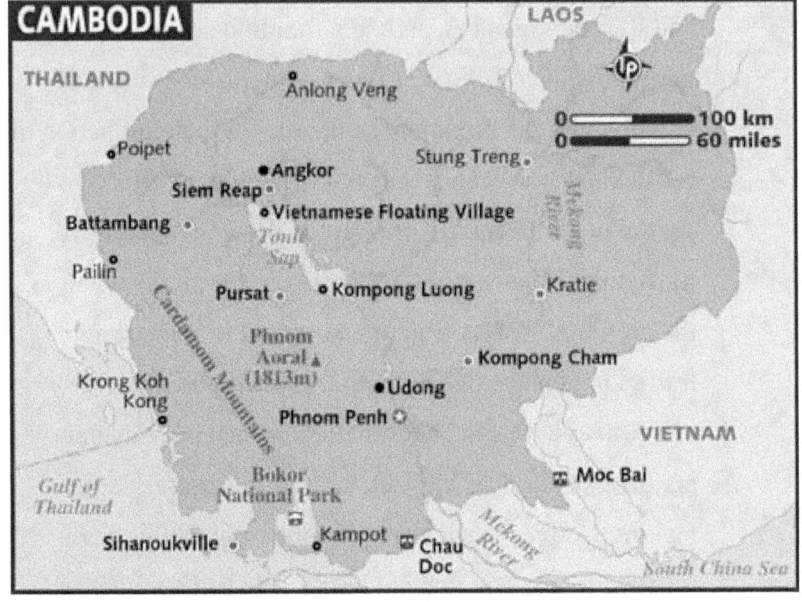

Other Key Facts™ Titles

Key Facts on South Korea

Key Facts on France

Key Facts on the United Kingdom

Key Facts on Egypt

Key Facts on Israel

All Key Facts™ Titles are Available at

www.Amazon.com

THE INTERNATIONALIST®

2014

WWW.INTERNATIONALIST.COM

www.ingramcontent.com/pod-product-compliance
Lightning Source LLC
Chambersburg PA
CBHW070716180526
45167CB00004B/1494